Chakapan Baba Ati
or
The Heart of Baba Malay

Buku 6

Book 6 - The Heart of Baba Malay

Chakapan Baba Ni Ari series

Baba Malay Today series

All Rights Reserved.
No part of this publication may be reproduced, stored in a retrieval system, or transmitted, in any form or by any means electronic, mechanical, photocopying, recording or otherwise, without the prior written permission of the publishers.

Theresa Fuller asserts the moral right to be identified as the author of this work.

Bare Bear Media

ISBN 978-1-925748-24-6 - Print
ISBN 978-1-925748-25-3 - Ebook

Cover by Helzkat Designs

Copyright May 2024©

Sincere thanks to my husband, Paul, who supported this work in every way possible. I love you.

Many thanks also to my proofreaders for their checking. Special mention to Tim Fuller and Rosalind Ang.

National Library of Australia
US Library of Congress

Published 24th of May 2024

Introduction - Essence

Language is powerful.

In writing this text, I applied the SHOW don't TELL method. I wanted the reader to be able to pick up this book and begin to learn. Much as you would pick up a game and play.

>Chobak.

>To try.

Unlike my previous books, this book is about what I have been told is the **heart** of Baba Malay - its essence. Besides Baba Malay being a fusion of Hokkien and Malay, there are 3 ways that differentate the Baba Malay speaker from a speaker of Malay i.e., Bahasa Melayu.

The 3 main ways are through the usage of:

1. Adjectives
2. Passive Voice, and
3. Relative Clauses

Plus a few extras.

Of course there will be some who disagree. Every family has their own rules. The main thing is to use Baba Malay in whatever way and don't worry if you make mistakes, or break any rules.

Use it. Or we will lose it.

Each day, try to have fun.

This is Baba Malay; the language of the Peranakans.

YOUR language.

Baba Malay

Baba Malay is the language of my ancestors.

A language that I discovered late in 2021 was about to go extinct with fewer than a thousand speakers in the world. I took a course in Baba Malay taught by Kenneth Chan, author of *BABA MALAY FOR EVERYONE - A comprehensive guide to the Peranakan language*. This was my start to saving Baba Malay.

But I believed much more had to be done.

The book you hold in your hands is the result of my mad persistence to save my language. While there are books out there on Baba Malay, I found little in the way for children. As a teacher, I believe that to save a language we must start with the young.

I wanted a book that parents could give to their children.
One I could give to my kids.

This is my attempt.

Theresa, affectionately known in the Peranakan community as Bibek Theresa.

Sydney,
29th of May, 2022

Iau Kin

Iau Kin = Important

in the Yunnan Province.

Contents

Introduction	3
Baba Malay	4
Adjectives in general	8
Chobak Adjectives	9
Positive, Comparative, Superlative	11
Revision	13
Introducing Adjectives in Baba Malay	23
Using Positive	24
Chobak Positive	29
Using Comparative	31
Sample Sentences	37
Chobak - Positive and Comparative in Baba Malay	40
Using Superlative	43
Sekali and Superlatives	46
Chobak Adjectives in Baba Malay	47
Introducing Active and Passive Voice	53
Passive Voice in Baba Malay	56
Passive Voice using Kasi or Kena	57
Chobak - Passive Voice	59
Introduction to Relative Clauses	63
Using Relative Clauses in Baba Malay	66
Chobak - Relative Clauses	68

His family came from Uzbekistan.

Tambah Sikit	71
The Baba Malay Alphabet	73
The Baba Malay Language Family Chart	75
William Girdlestone Shellabear	76
Tempu - Time	78
DAYS of the Week	78
DAYS of the Week showing Hokkien influence	79
Other Related Time Phrases	80
Telling Time	81
Question Particles - Tak and Kan	83
Salutations - Female	84
Salutations - Male	85
Pronunciation	86
Words used Differently	87
List of Adjectives	
A, B, C	88
D, E, F	89
G, H	90
I, K, L	91
M, N, O	92
P, Q, R	93
S, T	94
U, W, Y	95
Notes	96
About the Author	97
More books in the Baba Malay Today Series	98
Dear Reader	99
New Peranakan Tales Series	100

ADJECTIVES in general

Girl = Prompuan
She = Dia

Adjectives are words used to describe nouns and pronouns. Nouns are naming words. Pronouns are words like 'she' and 'he.'

    Girl = Noun
    She = Pronoun

Adding the adjective 'Happy' gives us: Happy girl. As you can see, this second girl is very different to the girl above.

    Girl = Prompuan
    He/She = Dia
    Happy = Senang Ati or Cheng Ati but not gembira

English   =   **Happy** girl. She is happy.

Baba Malay   =   Prompuan **senang ati**. Dia senang ati.
(In this simple example the adjective comes **AFTER** the noun.)

Adjectives can also be used by themselves e.g.,

Chantek! Mahair! Rajin!
Or Beautiful! Expensive! Clever!

CHOBAK - ADJECTIVES

Let's try a few adjectives: cute, sad, angry.

Cute = Chomel
Sad = Sayup
Angry = Marah

1. Cute girl.　　　　　　　　　　She is cute.
Answer: _____.　　　　_____.

2. Sad girl.　　　　　　　　　　She is sad.
Answer: _____.　　　　_____.

3. Angry girl.　　　　　　　　　She is angry.
Answer: _____.　　　　_____.
And we are back to the first girl again.

Answers: 1. Prompuan chomel. Dia chomel. 2. Prompuan sayup. Dia sayup. 3. Prompuan marah. Dia marah.

The Different Types of Adjectives

Man = Jantan
He/She = Dia

Adjectives describe objects.

Here are more examples of adjectives: clever, lazy, old.

    Clever man.   He is clever.
    Lazy man.   He is lazy.
    Old man.   He is old.

In Baba Malay, we get:

    Jantan **panday**. Dia panday.
    Jantan **malair**.   Dia malair.
    Jantan **tua**.   Dia tua.

But so far we are only describing one object. What if we need to describe more than one object?

Depending on the number of objects, we can use either a comparative or a superlative adjective. Don't worry. We use them all the time in English.

as their homeland was under invasion.

POSITIVE, COMPARATIVE, SUPERLATIVE

Blocks = Blocks

There are 3 types of adjectives: positive, comparative and superlative.

Which adjective to use depends on the number of objects being described.

Number of Objects being described:

1   - Use a **Positive Adjective**

2   - Use a **Comparative Adjective**

3 or more   - Use a **Superlative Adjective**

Please **NOTE**: Pages 12 to 22 are on revision of adjectives. If you have a comfortable grasp on adjectives, you may skip ahead to Page 23.

Revision

Revision of POSITIVE and COMPARATIVE Adjectives

Long hair, short hair = Rambot Panjang, Rambot Pendek

Adjectives provide a description i.e., information.

This is how they are generally used:

Positive Adjective - To describe 1 object

Just use the adjective e.g., **short, long.**

    Short hair. Long hair.

Comparative Adjective - To describe 2 objects

Add 'r' to the adjective e.g., cute**r**, base**r**.

or Add 'er' to the adjective e.g., short**er**, long**er**.

Sometimes you may also need to add the last letter of the word e.g., thin**n**er, fat**t**er.

    Thinner book. Fatter book.

    Or an 'i' e.g., skin**nier**.

    Skin**nier** child.

Revision of SUPERLATIVE Adjectives

Child = Adek

Superlative Adjective - To describe 3 or more objects

Add 'est' e.g., Short**est**, long**est**.

Shortest way. Longest way.

Sometimes you may also need to add the last letter of the word, e.g., Thi**nn**est, Fa**tt**est.

Thinnest book. Fattest book.

Or an 'i' e.g., skin**niest**.

Skinniest child.

Glossary

Book = Buku
Child = Adek
Fat = Gemok
Hair = Rambot
Long = Panjang
Short = Pendek
Thin, Skinny = Kurus

Using POSITIVE, COMPARATIVE, SUPERLATIVE to show an INCREASE

Adjectives: Fat, Fatter, Fattest
Example of increase

Positive Adjective
To describe 1 object.
One **young** person.

Comparative Adjective
To describe 2 objects.
Second young person.

Is the second young person younger than the first person?
Yes. The second person is **younger** than the first person.

Superlative Adjective
To describe 3 or more objects.
Here are three people.

The one on the far right is the **youngest**.

pilgrimages to Mecca.

Using POSITIVE, COMPARATIVE, SUPERLATIVE to show a DECREASE

Adjectives: Small, Smaller, Smallest
Example of decrease

Positive Adjective
To describe 1 object
Small chair.

Comparative Adjective
To describe 2 objects
Smaller chair

Is one chair smaller than the other?
Yes. The chair on the right is the **smaller** chair.

Superlative Adjective
To describe 3 or more objects
Smallest chair.

Is one chair smaller than the others?
Yes. The chair on the far right is the **smallest** chair.

Ma He was impressed with the exciting journeys.

Chobak - Positive, Comparative, Superlative - 'er' or 'est'

Tablets of different sizes

Dark, Darker, Darkest
Fair, Fairer, Fairest
Long, Longer, Longest
Tall, Taller, Tallest
Thin, Thinner, Thinnest
Short, Shorter, Shortest

The positives are: Dark, Fair, L_____, _____, _____, _____

The comparatives are: ____, Fairer, Longer, _____, _____, _____

The superlatives are: ____, ____, Longest, Tallest, _____, _____

Glossary

    Dark = Gelap
    Fair = Puteh
    Long = Panjang
    Tall = Tinggi
    Thin = Kurus
    Short = Pendek

Answers: Positives: Dark, Fair, Long, Tall, Thin, Short
          Comparatives: Darker, Fairer, Longer, Taller, Thinner, Shorter
          Superlatives: Darkest, Fairest, Longest, Tallest, Thinnest, Shortest

POSITIVE, COMPARATIVE, SUPERLATIVE
- 'more' or most'

Diamond = Belian

Sometimes, however, we cannot simply just add 'er' or 'est'.

We need to add 'more' or 'most' in front of the adjective.

Expensive = Mahair

POSITIVE:
Expensive diamond
This diamond is expensive.

COMPARATIVE:
More expensive diamond
This diamond is **more** expensive than the diamond above.
(Comparing 2 diamonds)

SUPERLATIVE:
Most expensive diamond
This diamond is the **most** expensive diamond of all the diamonds on this page.
(Comparing 3 or more)

POSTIVE, COMPARATIVE, SUPERLATIVE
- different adjectives

Many Houses = Banyak Rumah

And sometimes we need to use a completely different adjective altogether as in the following example:

    Good, Better, Best

The first house is a **good** house, but the house on the far right is a **better** house. The tallest house however is the **best** house.

Thankfully, this is never the case with Baba Malay. So examples like these below just don't happen:

    Bad, Worse, Worst
    Little, Less, Least
    Much, More, Most
    Far, Further/Farther, Furthest/Farthest

So how do we use adjectives in Baba Malay?

End of Revision

He must have dreamt that one day

Introducing ADJECTIVES in Baba Malay

Lesson = Ajairan

Generally there are:

    5 ways to use **POSITIVE**
    6 ways to use **COMPARATIVE**
    3 ways to use **SUPERLATIVE**

Let's learn what these ways are.

Using POSITIVE in Baba Malay - #1

Big Table = Meja Besair

1. Simply add the adjective:

    Baba Malay   =   Subject/Object + **Adjective**

                         Meja/Tok **besair**.

More examples

Thin man -> Laki kurus or Dia kurus.

Short man -> Laki pendek or Dia pendek.

or

Thin woman -> Prompuan kurus or Dia kurus.

Short woman -> Prompuan pendek or Dia pendek.

Glossary

Man = Laki
Short = Pendek
Thin = Kurus
Woman = Prompuan

His parents encouraged him.

Using POSITIVE in Baba Malay - #2

Big Tiger = Arimo besair

2. Or with the possessive 'mia' or 'nia' or 'punya'.

Baba Malay   =   **Adjective** + *Possessive* + Subject/Object

Besair *mia* arimo. Or **Besair** *punya* arimo.

More examples

Beautiful tiger -> Chantek punya arimo. Or Chantek mia arimo.
        (The tiger which owns beauty)
Brave tiger -> Brani mia arimo. Or Brani nia arimo.
        (Bravery belonging to the tiger)
or
Beautiful horse -> Chantek punya kuda. Or Chantek nia kuda.
Brave horse -> Brani mia kuda. Brani nia kuda.

Glossary

Beautiful = Chantek
Belonging to = Punya/Mia/Nia
Brave = Brani
Ownership = Punya/Mia/Nia

But war soon came to Yunnan.

Using POSITIVE in Baba Malay - #3

Small Horse = Kuda kechik

3. Or if we wish to **emphasise** the adjective, with the word 'yang'.

    Baba Malay   =   Subject/Object + Yang + **Adjective**

    Kuda yang **kechik**.

More examples

Strong horse -> Kuda yang kuat. (The horse which is strong.)
Fast horse -> Kuda yang chepat. (The horse which is fast)
or
Strong tiger -> Arimo yang kuat.
Fast tiger -> Arimo yang chepat.

Glossary

Fast = Chepat
Strong = Kuat
That, Which, Who = Yang

Using POSITIVE in Baba Malay - #4

Goldfish = Ikan mair

4. Or use the adjective by itself.

Baba Malay   =   **Adjective**

Besair.

More examples

What colour is that fish? Gold. -> Apa orna ikan tu? Mair.

What colour is that rabbit? White. -> Apa orna Kuching Belanda tu? Puteh.

Glossary

Colour = Orna
Fish = Ikan
Gold = Mair
Rabbit = Kuching Belanda
White = Puteh

Using POSITIVE in Baba Malay - #5

Rabbit = Kuching Belanda

5. Replicate the adjective. This is generally done for emphasis.

    Baba Malay   =   **Adjective + Adjective**

                                Besair-besair.

More examples

That rabbit runs fast. ->Kuching Belanda tu lari chepat-chepat.

Eh, walk slowly. -> Eh, jalan pelan-pelan.

He is a good boy -> Dia budak baik-baik.

Glossary

Cat = Kuching
Dutch = Belanda
Fast = Chepat
Good = Baik
Rabbit = Kuching Belanda(See Cat & Dutch)
Slow = Pelan-pelan

Worse was to come.

Chobak - POSITIVE

Rich = Kaya

Translate into Baba Malay: Rich person.

1. Add the adjective:

Baba Malay = _____.

2. With 'mia' or 'nia' or 'punya':

Baba Malay = _____.

3. With the word 'yang':

Baba Malay = _____.

4. Adjective by itself:

Baba Malay = _____.

5. Replicated:

Baba Malay = _____.

Answers: 1. Orang kaya. 2. Kaya mia orang. 3. Orang yang kaya. 4. Kaya. 5. Kaya-kaya.

Chobak - POSITIVE

Poor = Miskin

Translate into English: Poor man.

1. Add the adjective:

Orang Miskin = _____.

2. With 'mia' or 'nia' or 'punya':

Miskin mia orang = _____.

3. With the word 'yang':

Orang yang miskin. = _____.

4. Adjective by itself:

Miskin. = _____.

5. Replicated:

Miskin = _____.

Answers: 1. Poor man. 2. The man who owns poverty. 3. The man who/which is poor. 4. Poor. 5. Poor-poor. Eg., This poor poor man.

Then Ma He himself was captured.

Using COMPARATIVE in Baba Malay - #1
- more

This table is more big  than this table.

1. For More or Greater:

Baba Malay = Subject 1 + Lagik/Lebeh (more) + **Adjective** + Lagik (Than) + Subject 2

> Ni meja lagik besair lagik ni meja.
> Ni meja lebeh besair lagik ni meja.

More examples

Fried noodles are more delicious than blanched noodles.
->   Mee goreng lagik sedap lagik mee rebus.
       Mee goreng lebih sedap lagik mee rebus.

or

Water is more tasteless than milk.
->   Ayer lagik tawar lagik susu.
       Ayer lebih tawar lagik susu.

Glossary

Blanched = Rebus
Delicious = Sedap
Fried = Goreng
Milk = Susu
Noodles = Mee
Tasteless = Tawar
Water = Ayer

He was castrated.

Using COMPARATIVE in Baba Malay - #2
- less

This table is less big **than this table.**

2. For Less:

> Baba Malay = Subject 1 + Kurang (less) + **Adjective** + Lagik (Than) + Subject 2
>
> Ni meja/tok kurang besair lagik ni meja.

More examples

> This blue dress is less expensive than that red dress.
> -> Baju biru ni kurang harga lagik baju merah tu.
>
> or
>
> Today's weather is less cold than yesterday's weather.
> -> Cuacha ari ni kurang sejuk lagik cuacha semalam.

Glossary

> Cold = Sejuk
> Today = Ari ni
> Weather = Cuacha
> Yesterday = Semalam

Using COMPARATIVE in Baba Malay - #3
- quantity

Marbles = Guli

I have more marbles than you.

3. For Quantity (Many ways to do this):

Baba Malay = Ada + Lagik + Manyak + Noun + Lagik + Subject/Object

        Gua ada lagik manyak guli lagik lu.

More examples

My house has more rooms than yours.
-> Gua mia rumah ada lagik manyak bilek lagik lu mia rumah.

or

Sally has read more books than Sue.
-> Sally ada bacha lagik manyak buku lagik Sue.

or

Sally has read two more books than Sue.
-> Sally ada bacha dua lagik manyak buku lagik Sue.

Glossary
    Book = Buku
    Read = Bacha
    Room = Bilek

Using COMPARATIVE in Baba Malay - #4
- by itself

Terrapin = Kikura

My terrapin is more cute.

4. Without referring to the second comparative:

Baba Malay = Subject/Object + Lagik + **Adjective**

Saya mia kikura lagik chomel.

More examples

My house is more beautiful.- > Gua mia rumah lagik chantek.

or

My dog is bigger. - > Gua mia anjing lagik besair.

Glossary

Beautiful = Chantek
Cute = Chomel
House = Rumah
Very = Sekali (Adverb)

Using COMPARATIVE in Baba Malay - #5
- Comparision of equality

Drum = Tambor

This drum is as noisy as that drum.

5. Comparison of Equality:

Baba Malay = Subject 1 + **Adjective** + Sama + Subject 2

Tambor ni bising sama tambor tu.

More examples

This popiah is as delicious as that chapchye.
-> Popiah ni sedap sama chapchye tu.

or

This pickles is as sour as those pickles.
-> Achar ni assam sama achar tu.

Glossary

Delicious = Sedap
Pickles = Achar
Sour = Assam

Using COMPARATIVE in Baba Malay - #6
- Comparision of similarity

Marbles = Guli

He is almost as rich as his brother.

6. Comparison of Similarity(Almost alike):

Baba Malay = Subject 1 + **Adjective** + Begi/Macham + Subject 2

Dia kaya macham dia mia hia.

More examples

Cold as ice. -> Sejuk begi air batu.

or

Dry as a bone -> Kering macham tulang.

Glossary

Bone = Tulang
Cold = Sejuk = Cold
Dry = Kering
Ice = Ayer Batu

Sample Sentences

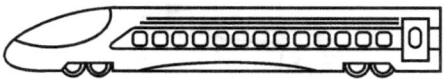

Train = Kreta Api

English	Baba Malay
This is a fast train.	Kreta api ni chepat.
This train is more fast than this car.	Kreta api ni lagik chepat lagik kreta ni.
This train is long.	Kreta api ni panjang.
This train is more long than this car.	Kreta api ni lebeh panjang lagik kreta ni.
That horse is less big than that horse.	Kuda tu kurang besair lagik kuda tu.
I have three more cats than you.	Gua ada tiga lagik kuching lagik lu.
This day is hotter.	Ari ni lagik panair.
This fruit is as sweet as sugar.	Kueh ni manis sama gula.
Clever as the mousedeer.	Panday macham kanchel.

Sample Sentences

Car = Kreta

Using the possessive 'mia' or 'punya':

English	Baba Malay
This is the train which owns speed.	Ni chepat mia kreta api.
This is the car to which speed belongs.	Ni chepat mia kreta.
Speed belongs to this train.	Ni chepat punya kreta api.
This is the car which owns fastness.	Ni chepat punya kreta.

Sample Sentences

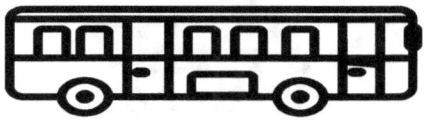

Bus = Bair

Using the word 'yang'.

English	Baba Malay
This is the bus which is speedy.	Ni bair yang chepat.
This is the bus which is fast.	Ni bair yang chepat.

CHOBAK - POSITIVE & COMPARATIVE in Baba Malay

Low House = Rumah Rendah

Translate the following into Baba Malay

1. This house is big.

2. This house is small.

3. This house is tall.

4. This house is low.

5. This house is average sized.

6. This house is more big than that house.

7. This house is less big than this house.

8. This house is more small than this house.

9. Anne's house is average sized.

10. Clara's house is big. Her house is bigger than mine.

11. My house is small. My house is smaller than Eloise's house.

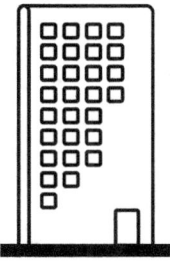

Tall House = Rumah Tinggi

12. This house is average in size. My house is smaller than the average house. But it is prettier.

13. The elephant is bigger.

14. The mousedeer to which cleverness belongs.

15. Work hard.

Glossary

Beautiful = Chantek
Big = Besair
Clever = Panday
Elephant = Gajah
House = Rumah
Medium = Sedang-sedang
Mousedeer = Kanchel
Short = Rendah
Small = Kechik
Tall = Tinggi

Answers on the next page.

In the palace,

Answers

1. Ni rumah besair.

2. Ni rumah kechik.

3. Ni rumah tinggi.

4. Ni rumah rendah.

5. Ni rumah sedang-sedang.

6. Ni rumah lagik besair lagik rumah tu.

7. Ni rumah kurang besair lagik ni rumah.

8. Ni rumah lagik kechik lagik ni rumah.

9. Anne mia rumah sedang-sedang.

10. Clara mia rumah besair. Dia mia rumah lebeh besair lagik gua mia rumah.

11. Saya mia rumah kechik. Saya mia rumah lagik kechik lagik Eloise mia rumah.

12. Ni rumah sedang-sedang. Gua mia rumah lagik kechik lagik rumah sedang-seadng. Tapi gua mia rumah lagik chantek.

13. Gajah lagik besair.

14. Kanchel yang cherdek.

15. Kerja kuat-kuat.

Using SUPERLATIVE in Baba Malay - #1

Story = Chrita

This is the saddest story.

1. Based on previous comparative:

Baba Malay = Subject/Object + Yang + **Adjective** + Sekali

> Chrita yang sedeh sekali.
> Literally = Story which is saddest very.

More examples

Noon is the hottest time of the day. -> Tempu tengah ari tempu yang panair sekali.

or

Examination which is the hardest of all. -> Pereksa yang susah sekali.

Please NOTE: There are always exceptions.

As much as I have tried to present the rules, there are often exceptions with the way Baba Malay is spoken. To present a superlative, indirect clauses are often used.

Using SUPERLATIVE in Baba Malay - #2

Song = Lagu

This is the easiest song.

1. Using the phrase 'Yang Abis':

> Baba Malay = Subject/Object + Yang Abis + **Adjective**
>
> Lagu yang abis senang.
> Literally = Song which finished as the easiest.

More examples

This is the news that shocked me the most. -> Ni khabar yang abis terperanjat saya.

or

That is the gift that is the best of all. -> Tu buah tangan yang abis baik.

Glossary
Gift = buah tangan
News = Khabar
Shocked/Startled = Terperanjat
Song = Lagu
That, Which, Who = Yang/Nan/Nang

Using SUPERLATIVE in Baba Malay - #3

Giant = Gergasi

This is the tallest giant.

1. Excessive Degree:

Baba Malay = Subject/Object + Terlalu + **Adjective**

        Gergasi terlalu panjang.
    Literally = The giant that is surpassing tall.

More examples

Chilli that is too hot. -> Chilli terlalu panair.
(Or Chilli that surpasses hotness.)

or

Person who surpasses all in lateness. -> Orang terlalu lambat.

Glossary

    Giant = Gergasi, Gergasang, Girgasi (many ways to spell.)
    Hot = Panair
    Very or surpassing = Terlalu

SEKALI and Superlatives

Princess = Puteri

Sekali is derived from **'Kali'** which means times or instances.

> Satu kali = Once or One time.
> Dua kali = Twice or Two times.
> Sekali = One time. However, when used with adjectives can denote superlative.

First example (denoting the number of times)

> I went to Australia **once** - > Saya pi Australia **satu kali**.

Second example (denoting superlative)

> The Princess of Gunung Ledang surpasses all in beauty. -> Puteri Gunung Ledang chantek **sekali.**

> As seen in Superlative in Baba Malay #1 on page 43, sekali takes on the meaning of 'very'.

Glossary

> Beauty = Chantek
> Mount = Gunung
> Orphir = Ledang
> Princess = Puteri
> Went = Pi

he was chosen

CHOBAK - ADJECTIVES in Baba Malay

Bear = Beruang

Translate the following into Baba Malay

1. This is the house of the Three Bears.

2. Papa Bear is bigger than Mama Bear.

3. Mama Bear is smaller than Papa Bear.

4. Baby Bear is the smallest bear.

5. The Three Bears love to eat porridge.

6. Papa Bear's porridge is the hottest.

7. Mama Bear's porridge is the coldest.

8. Baba Bear's porridge is the most delicious.

9. Papa Bear's chair is harder than Mama Bear's chair.

10. Mama Bear's chair is softer than Papa Bear's chair.

Answers on the next page.

Answers

1. Ni rumah Beruang Tiga mia rumah.

2. Beruang Pak lagik besair lagik Beruang Mak.

3. Beruang Mak lebeh kechik lagik Beruang Pak.

4. Beruang Anak yang kechik sekali.

5. Beruang Tiga suka makan bubor.

6. Beruang Pak mia bubor yang panair sekali.

7. Beruang Mak mia bubor yang sejuk sekali.

8. Beruang Anak mia bubor yang abis sedap.

9. Beruang Pak mia kerosi lebeh kerair lagik Beruang Mak mia kerosi.

10. Beruang Mak mia kerosi kurang kerair lagik Beruang Pak mia kerosi.

Glossary

Cold = Sejuk,
Hard = Kerair or Keras
Porridge = Bubor
Soft = Lembek

CHOBAK - ADJECTIVES in Baba Malay

Pig = Babi

Translate the following into English

1. Ni rumah Babi Tiga mia rumah.

2. Ni rumah straw.

3. Ni rumah kayu.

4. Rumah batu lebeh kerair lagik rumah kayu.

5. Rumah kayu lebeh kerair lagik rumah straw.

6. Rumah straw kurang kerair lagik rumah kayu.

7. Rumah kayu lebeh lembek lagik rumah batu.

8. Bacon yang abis sedap.

9. Straw yang lembek sekali.

10. Batu yang kerair sekali.

Answers on the next page.

Answers

1. This house is the house of the Three Pigs.

2. This is a house of straw.

3. This is a house of wood or This is a wooden house.

4. The brick house is stronger than the wooden house.

5. The house of wood is stronger than the house of straw.

6. The house of straw is not as strong as the house of wood.

7. The house of wood is less strong than the house of brick.

8. Bacon is most delicious.

9. Straw is the weakest.

10. Brick is the toughest.

Glossary

Baby = Anak
Delicious = Sedap
Hard = Kerair or Keras
Wood = Kayu

the emperor rewarded him.

INTRODUCING ACTIVE and PASSIVE VOICE

Coconut and Egg Jam = Kaya
(Kaya can also mean rich. And no, you don't get rich eating kaya.)

What is Active and Passive Voice?
Let's define first what is Active Voice.

Here is a typical everyday sentence:

> Theresa loves kaya.

Breaking up the sentence into 3 parts, we get:

> Theresa = Subject
> Loves = Verb
> Kaya = Object

The Subject (Theresa) performs the action.

The Action performed is shown by the verb (loves).

The Object (kaya) is what was acted on.

So because the subject (Theresa) is doing the action, this sentence is said to be in the active voice.

NOTE: Not all sentences need an object e.g., Theresa ate.

Nonya Spicy Pickled Vegetables = Achar

So what is Passive Voice?

Let's look at the same sentence:

>Theresa loves kaya.

In Passive Voice, the word order is changed. And the subject is no longer active but is instead acted upon by the verb.

So... we simply move the sentence's direct object into the subject field.

>Kaya is loved by Theresa.

Further examples:

>Jonathan rides horses. (Active)
>Horses are ridden by Jonathan. (Passive)
>
>Peranakans eat achar.
>Achar is eaten by Peranakans.

It is not the intention of this book to teach English grammar, so please refer to other texts if you are interested in the various forms of Active and Passive Voice.

To Bake = Bengka

Active Voice example ->   Sally baked a cake.

Subject = Sally (The performer doing the baking)

    Verb   = baked

    Object = cake

English Passive Voice ->   A cake was baked by Sally.

The Passive Voice is often used when we want to emphasize something other than the performer of the action.

More examples:

Tara played a card game. - Active

A card game was played by Tara. - Passive

Hudson climbed a wall. - Active

A wall was climbed by Hudson. - Passive

PASSIVE VOICE in Baba Malay

Play card game = Main terop

While the Passive Voice emphasizes something other than the performer of the action, in Baba Malay we go one step further and remove the performer.

    English Passive Voice   ->   A cake was baked by him.

    Baba Malay Passive Voice   ->   A cake was baked.

More examples:

A card game was played.

A wall was climbed.

In the above examples, it is unimportant as to who did the action.

Lastly, to express the Passive Voice in Baba Malay, we also need to use the terms 'kasi' or 'kena.'

PASSIVE VOICE using Kasi or Kena

Red Apple = Jambu Chili

Basically, use **kasi** in all circumstances unless...
antagonistic, adverse or opposing as **kena** is an adversative passive.

    Kasi = To Give
    Kena = To Hit (Experienced)

Passive Voice in English -> The apple was eaten.

Passive Voice in Baba Malay -> Jambu Chili kasi makan.
(Kasi) (Literal translation) -> The red apple give to be eaten.
i.e., (Actual meaning) The red apple gave itself to be eaten.

Passive Voice in Baba Malay -> Jambu Chili kena churi.
(Kena)   The red apple experienced or was subjected to being stolen.

In those days,

Durian = Durian

Passive Voice in English -> The durian was bought.

Passive Voice in Baba Malay -> Durian kasi beli.
    (Kasi) (Literal translation) -> The durian was purchased.

Passive Voice in Baba Malay -> Ikan kena tangkap.
    (Kena)   The fish was caught.

More examples:

    The dress was worn.

    This cake was baked.

    The holiday was taken.

envoys would arrive at the emperor's court.

Chobak - Passive Voice

Mandarin Jacket = Baju Lok Chuan
Use Kena or Kasi

1. The building was built.

2. The porridge was cooked.

3. The wood was bought.

4. The stone was dropped.

5. The baby was loved.

6. The child was scolded.

7. The girl was bullied.

8. The money was stolen.

9. The man was cheated.

10. The Mandarin Jacket was torn.

Answers on the next page.

Answers

1. Rumah kasi naikkan.

2. Bubor kasi masakkan.

3. Kayu kasi beli.

4. Batu kasi jatoh.

5. Anak kasi sayang.

6. Anak kena maki.

7. Anak prompuan kena chiak pi.

8. Duit kena churi.

9. Orang laki kena lanyak.

10. Baju Lok Chuan kena koyak.

Introduction to RELATIVE CLAUSES

Green Apples = Jambu-jambu ijo

Relative Clauses (also known as adjective clauses) function like adjectives. They describe either a noun or a noun phrase.

Examples of nouns (naming word):

    apple, girl, table

Noun phrases are groups of words that contain a noun along with its modifier. They can be replaced by a pronoun.

Examples of noun phrases:

    The apple ('The' is a Modifier; 'Apple' is a noun.)

    An apple ('An' is a Modifier; 'Apple' is a noun.)

    One apple ('One' is a Modifier.)

    Delicious, red apples ('Delicious' and Red' are Modifiers.)

    Bright, young girl

Introduction to RELATIVE CLAUSES

Wooden Table = Meja Kayu

Examples of relative clauses:

> I ate an apple **which was delicious**.
> (relative phrase to describe a noun)
>
> I met a bright, young girl **who was wonderful**.
> (describing a noun phrase.)
>
> I purchased a shiny, wooden table **that I loved**.
> (describing a noun phrase.)

But Emperor Chengdu only had one man in mind.

Introduction to RELATIVE CLAUSES continued

Cooked Food = Masakan

As you can see from the examples on the previous page, a Relative Clause always begins with a relative pronoun e.g., who, whom, whose, that, and which.

I ate an apple **WHICH** was delicious.

Relative Clauses provide more information about another noun or a noun phrase.

I made a cake. **The cake** is delicious.

I made a cake **which** was delicious.

Glossary

Bake = Bengka
Embok-embok = Female aspect of the Peranakans
Laok = Food, Laok Embok-embok = Peranakan Food
Masak = Cook
Tok = Table

Using RELATIVE CLAUSES in Baba Malay

Shop = Keday

1. Using 'YANG' i.e., which:

Baba Malay = Noun/Noun Phrase + Yang + **Additional Description**

I want to cook Peranakan food **which is very delicious**.

Saya mo masak laok embok-embok yang **sedap sekali**.

Examples of relative clauses using 'yang':

This is my younger sister **who is beautiful**.

Ni saya mia adek prompuan **yang chantek**.

That is the shop **that sells sarong kebaya**.

Tu keday **yang juair sarong kebaya**.

I want to cook Peranakan food which is very delicious for a feast.

Saya mo masak laok embok-embok yang **sedap sekali** buat Tok Panjang.

Using RELATIVE CLAUSES in Baba Malay Continued

Feast = Tok Panjang

2. Using 'PUNYA' or 'MIA

Baba Malay = **Additional Description + PUNYA/IA(Which)** + Noun/Noun Phrase.

I want to cook Peranakan food **which is very delicious**.

Saya mo masak **sedap sekali punya** laok embok-embok.

Examples of relative clauses using 'punya' or 'mia.'

Ni gua mia **chantek punya** adek prompuan.

Tu **juair sarong kebaya punya** keday.

Saya mo masak **sedap sekali punya** laok embok-embok buat Tok Panjang.

Please NOTE: All Peranakans believe that Peranakan food is very delicious. To differ is to risk ire.

Chobak - Relative Clauses

School = Sekolah

Use Yang and then Punya or Mia

1. The school that I took my exams.

2. Places which I have never been.

3. Aunt whom I have never met.

4. Grandfather whose house this is.

5. My friend whose dress I have borrowed.

(Please NOTE: There are always exceptions.)

Answers on opposite page.

Answers - Relative Clauses

Exam = Pereksa

Using Yang

1. Sekolah yang saya ambek saya mia pereksa.

2. Tempat-tempat yang saya tak pernah pi.

3. Koko/Ee Ee yang saya tak pernah jumpa.

4. Kong Kong yang sapa mia rumah ni.

5. Gua mia kawan yang baju saya pinjam

Using Punya or Mia

1. Saya ambek saya mia pereksa punya sekolah.

2. Saya tak pernah pi punya tempat-tempat.

3. Saya tak pernah jumpa mia Koko/Ee Ee.

4. Kong-kong sapa mia punya rumah ni.

5. Saya mia kawan punya baju saya pinjam.

Tambah sikit
Extra little

The Baba Malay Alphabet

A, B, C, D, E, F, G, H, I, J, K, L, M, N, O, P, R, S, T, U, W, Y & Z.

22 or 23 letters?

Baba Malay in 1913 was the mother-tongue of the Chinese women and children in the Straits Settlements and of a multitude in the Federated Malay States according to W. G. Shellabear, who also said:

"It is sure to live."

Sadly, today Baba Malay is fighting to survive.

Baba Malay was also mainly an oral language with more than one way to pronounce or to spell certain words.

Going by William Gwee's dictionary - a baba malay dictionary - there are apparently 22 letters in the Baba Malay alphabet. I say apparently because there is no word beginning with the letter 'f' in his dictionary.

I have since found 2 words:

> Faida = Faedah (Standard Malay), Interest (English)
> Feshen = Fashion

The first word was found in Pantun Pilihan Peranakan Baba Negeri Selat 1910-1930, edited by Ding Choo Ming while the second word was found in Shellabear's writing.

Of course, this is not to say that 'f' is not used in spelling.

Accoding to Nala Lee, A GRAMMAR OF MODERN BABA MALAY, Baba Malay is a contact language which has multiple influences:

Very broad definition:

>Sinitic + Austronesian

Narrower defintion:

>Southern Min + Malayic

Please note that the definitions below are very, very simplified. I am not a linguist. Any errors are mine.

Austronesian = A language family widely spoken throughout Maritime SE Asia (the old name for maritime SE Asia was Nusantara);

Contact Language = A marginal language used for the purposes of communication between two or more people who have no common language;

Dravidian language = spoken mainly in southern India, NE Sri Lanka & SW Pakistan;

Indo-European language = spoken by the majority of Europe, the Iranian plateau, and the northen Indian subcontinent. The Germanic languages are one of its branches: North Germanic, West Germanic and East Germanic;

Southern Min = A group of linguistically similar and historically related Chinese languages that form a branch of Min Chinese spoken in Fujian;

which was what the junks were named.

Malayic = Branch of the Malayo-Polynesian subgroup of the Austronesian language family;

Sinitic language = synonymous with the Chinese languages;

I would have loved to have been able to obtain a diagram but have been told that none exists. I then tried to produce one but apparently a family tree diagram would not suffice.

Is Baba Malay (BBM) a language or a dialect etc?

I leave that argument to the linguists. My main aim has always been to save *Baba Malay*, whatever *it* may be.

Baba Malay has adopted words from English, Portuguese, Dutch and Tamil while also incorporating grammatical characteristics of its component languages. Please refer to Lee's A GRAMMAR OF MODERN BABA MALAY for a more indepth understanding.

And as for how the term 'Baba' came about?

I had my suspicion that Baba might have been the Chinese for father so I was very glad to read Lee's explanation on page 21 of her book that it is possibly an unaspirated [p] therefore sounding more like a [b].

Hence, Baba Malay is virtually Father's Malay.

And as for who discovered it being used?

W. G. Shellabear
(1862-1947)

Liu Jia Harbour in Jiangsu province and

William Girdlestone Shellabear

W. G. Shellabear was born in 1862 at Holkham Hall, Norfolk, England. He arrived initially in Malaya as a British soldier, but returned later as a Methodist missionary. He founded the MPH (Methodist Publishing House) Group.

Shellabear noticed the different types of Malay being spoken in Malaya, Java and other parts of the Netherlands Indies. It was he who identified Baba Malay as a quite distinct dialect being spoken by the Malay-speaking Chinese.

"It is the language of the homes of the Straits-born Chinese - the most highly educated and the most influential section of the Chinese community in the British possessions, and therefore it is the language on which the women and children of this important class can most readily and most successfully be educated... Baba Malay is the language of the man of the street; it is a strong and virile tongue, more easily acquired than the pure Malay, and sufficiently expressive for all ordinary purposes; moreover it has a remarkable capacity for borrowing and assimilating such words as it needs from other languages."

- W. G. Shellabear -

TEMPU - TIME
DAYS of the Week

Here is a great example of how the Peranakans have utilised Hokkien grammar and Malay words to come up with their own way of expressing the days of the week.

In Malay, we have:

      Monday = Isnin
      Tuesday = Selasa
      Wednesday = Rabu
      Thursday = Khamis
      Friday = Jumaat
      Saturday = Sabtu
      Sunday = Ahad

Hari ini hari apa? What day is it?
Hari ini hari Ahad. Today is Sunday.

In Mandarin Chinese, we have:

      Monday = Week(Xingqi) Yi(One)
      Tuesday = Week(Xingqi) Er(Two)
      Wednesday = Week(Xingqi) San(Three)
      Thursday = Week(Xingqi) Si(Four)
      Friday = Week(Xingqi) Wu(Five)
      Saturday = Week(Xingqi) Liu(Six)
      Sunday = Week(Xingqi) Ri(Sun)/Tian(Heaven/Sky)

Jintian shi xingqi ji? = What day of the week is this?
Jintian shi Xingqi Tian. = Today is Sunday.

as the starting ports.

TEMPU
DAYS of the Week showing Hokkien influence

But our ancestors were mainly Hokkien, and so we have:

    Monday = Pai Yit (One)
    Tuesday = Pai Dee (Two)
    Wednesday = Pai Sah (Three)
    Thursday = Pai See (Four)
    Friday = Pai Gor (Five)
    Saturday = Pai Luck (Six)
    Sunday = Lay Pai

Pai = 拜

Pai = Certain day in a week. The Chinese character supposedly means a ritual of reverence, submission, worship, and paying respect.

And thus we have the Days of the Week, in Baba Malay:

    Monday = Ari Satu
    Tuesday = Ari Dua
    Wednesday = Ari Tiga
    Thursday = Ari Ampat
    Friday = Ari Lima
    Saturday = Ari Anam
    Sunday = Ari Minggu

Ni ari apa? What day is it?
Ni ari Ari Minggu. Today is Sunday.

TEMPU
Other Related Time Phrases

Afternoon = Tengah Hari
Always = Selalu
At times = Kadang Kali
Before = Dulu
Early = Siang-siang
Every = Tiap-tiap
Everyday = Ari-ari
Every morning = Pagi-pagi
Four days ago = Ampat ari lalu
How often = Berapa kali
In the past = Dulu
Just now = Tadik
Last night = Semalam malam
Late = Lambat
Later = Nanti
Morning = Pagi
Never = Tak pernah
Night = Malam
Not usually = Tak Biasa
Now or Later = Sekarang
Rarely = Jarang
Sooner or later = Chepat sama lambat (Idiom)
Sometimes = Kadang-kadang
Then = Lalu
Today = Ni Ari
Tomorrow = Besok
Three days ago = Kemaren dulu
Two days ago = Kemaren
Usually = Biasa
Yesterday = Semalam

Please NOTE satu ari means 1 day while Ari Satu means Monday

Amid exploding fire crackers,

TEMPU
Telling Time

1. We tell time by the hour, minute as well as the part of the day:

    Pukol satu pagi -> 1:00 am

    Pukol satu tengah hari -> 1:00 pm

2. We add the part of the day, to show am or pm:

    Ni jam pukol dua pagi -> It's 2:00 am

    Ni jam pukol tuju malam -> It's 7:00 pm

3. We can add minutes:

    Ni jam pukol tiga, lima pagi -> It's 3:05 am

    Ni jam pukol tuju, sepuloh malam -> It's 7:10 pm

4. We use time expressions:

    Ni jam pukol ampat suku -> It's 4:15

    Ni jam pukol lapan tengah -> It's 8:30

    Ni jam pukol semilan tiga-suku -> It's 9:45

5. We use BERAPA, to ask for the time:

    Pukol berapa? -> What time is it?
    (Literally o'clock how much?)

(Continued on the next page.)

the fleet set sail.

TEMPU

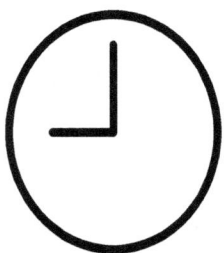

Clock = Aloji

6. We use BERAPA, to ask time related questions:

> Pukol berapa sekolah abis? -> What time does school finish?
>
> Pukol berapa Mak mo pi pasair? -> What time does Mother want to go to the market?
>
> Pukol berapa ni jam? -> What time is it now?

Glossary

>   Day = Hari or Ari
>   Half = Tengah
>   Hour = Jam
>   O'clock = Pukol
>   Quarter = Suku
>   Midday or Noon = Tengah Hari
>   Morning = Pagi
>   Night = Malam
>   Time = Jam
>   What = Berapa

QUESTION PARTICLES - Tak and Kan

Answer = Jawab

1. We add these at the end of YES/NO questions.

Add TAK if the speaker doesn't know the answer.

Mo pi, tak? -> Do you want to go, or not? (Literally.)
　　　　　　Do you want to go?

Lu mo beli, tak? ->Do you want to buy, or not? (Literally.)
　　　　　　Do you want to buy?

Add KAN if the speaker expects the answer to be yes based on shared assumptions.

Mo makan, kan? -> Do you want to eat, or not? (Literally.)
　　　　　　Do you want to eat?

Lu mo belajair, kan? ->Do you want to study, or not? (Literally.)
　　　　　　Do you want to study?

SALUTATIONS - Female

Greet/Call out = Teriak

Elder Sister - Tachi (Can also be used as a term of respect or closeness)
E.g., Tachi Linda

Auntie or Madam - Bibek

Miss or Ms or Mrs - Nonya. (Salutation commonly used among younger women, normally unmarried however also used by married women.)
Nya is the short form used among familiars

Mrs - Bibek. (Salutation commonly used among either older or married peranakan females.)

Younger Sister - Adek
E.g., Adek Rose

Salutation for a venerated Peranakan female - Wa-wak or Wak-wak.
(Probably the equivalent of the English Dame.)

Salutation for all reference to the female aspect of Baba Nonya culture e.g. Nonya cuisine. The term Laok embok-embok = Nonya Cuisine.

Embok means a Nonya lady.

SALUTATIONS - Male

Tabek = Salute/Greet

Elder Brother - Hia (blood relation) or Ng Ko
        Ng Ko can also be used to either as a sign of courtesy or respect

Uncle -   Inchek or Inche

Mister/Mr -   Baba. (Salutation used without reference to age.)
        Ba is the short form used among familiars or those younger than the speaker.

        Inchek or Inche (Salutation for males regardless of their age.)

Younger Brother - Adek
        E.g., Adek James

Baba tends to be the salutation for all reference of the Baba culture e.g., Baba Malay, the language of the Peranakans.

No male equivalent to Wa-wak.

Pronunciation

Speak = Chakap

According to William Gwee (A BABA MALAY DICTIONARY):

Generally words that end in 'a' are pronounced as 'ah'.

So lupa is pronounced lupah. Kena becomes kenah.

Words that end in 'al' or 'ar' or 'as' are pronounced as 'air'.

So tampal is pronounced tampair. Lebar becomes lebair.

Words that end in 'au' are pronounced as 'o'.

So pisau is pronounced and spelt piso; Kerbau becomes kerbo.

Words that begin with 'h' usually have the 'h' removed.

So hijo becomes ijo.

According to Felix Chia (THE BABAS):

Words such as 'abuk' meaning dust become 'abok'. Aversion for the 'u'.

Preference of 'e' to 'i' so adik becomes adek.

(Note: Please refer to Gwee's and Chia's books for more examples.)

Thanks to the Monsoon,

WORDS used Differently

Take note = Sedairkan

The Baba Malay language takes its grammar from Hokkien and most of its vocabulary from Malay but in the case of certain words, the Peranakans have taken them and made them their own.

This is often the case in language where terms can mean one thing to one culture, and something completely different in another. This is what car manufacturers watch out for when they name a new car.

Let's look at some words:

> **Mari** - In Malay, this word means 'come', but in Baba Malay, when 'mari' is used with an expression of invitation, it means 'please.'
>
> Please come. Mari Datang.
>
> **Saya** - I, myself or 'yes'.
>
> **Pasair** - Market or because. Always look at the context.
>
> **Sama-sama** - In Malay, this word means 'equally', but in Baba Malay it means "You're welcome."

(Note: Again refer to Gwee's and Chia's books for further examples.)

List of Adjectives

A

Aged = Tua
Arrogant = Lawa
Average-sized = Sedang-sedang

B

Bad = Jahat
Bald = Botak
Beautiful = Chantek
Big = Besair
Bitter = Pait
Black (Colour) = Itam
Blind = Buta
Blue (Colour) = Biru
Brave = Brani
Bright = Terang
Brown (Colour)= Chocolate

C

Cheap = Murah
Clean = Bersih
Clever = Panday
Coarse = Kasair [Kasar]
Cold = Sejok
Contented = Senang Ati

D

Dark = Gelap
Delicate = Alus
Delicious = Sedap
Demure = Lau sit
Difficult = Susah
Diligent = Rajin
Dilute = Chayer
Dirty = Kotor
Discontented = Susah Ati
Divine = Sakti
Dry = Kering

E

Early = Siang
Easy = Senang
Easy Going = Chin Chai
Evil = Jahat
Expensive = Mahair

F

Faded in apperance = Chomot
Fast = Chepat
Famous = Chut mia, Mashohor
Female = Prompuan
Fine = Alus
Forever = Selama-lama
Fussy = Kewat

G

Generous = Murah Ati
Gentle = Lemah-lembut
Giant = Gergasi, (Many ways to spell gergasi) Jin

Gold = Mair
Good = Baik
Green = Ijo

H

Happy = Senang Ati, Cheng Ati
Hard = Kuat
High = Tinggi
Hot = Panair
Hot-tempered = Panair Ati

I

Ill = Saket, but when ill, you say tak senang badan
Ill-tempered = Pai Piak
Important = Iau Kin
Improper Behaviour = Tak Seronoh
Intense = Kuat
Itchy = Gatal

K

Kind = Ati Baik

L

Late = Lambat
Lazy = Malair
Lean and lanky = Kurus Kering
Left = Kiri
Long = Panjang
Low = Rendah
Lowest Price = Putus Harga
Lucky = Naseb Baik

M

Magical = Sakti
Male = Jantan
Messy = Semak

N

Naughty = Nakair
Narrow = Sempet
Near = Dekat
Neat = Kemas
New = Baru
Noisy = Bising
No need = Toksa
Not up to Standard = Tak Sepekah

O

Obedient = Kuai
Old = Tua
Orange = Jingga

P

Patient = Sabair
Pock-marked = Bopeng
Polite = Tau Adat
Poor = Miskin
Purple (Colour) = Unggu
Pregnant = Duduk Perut
Pretty = Chantek
Proud = Lawa

Q

Quickly = Lekair-lekair
Quiet = Diam

R

Red = Merah
Right = Kanan
Round = Bulat
Rude = Kurang Ajair

S

Sad = Sedeh
Sadness = Sayup
Salty = Asin
Severe = Terok
Short = Pendek
Shy = Malu, Segan
Sick = Saket
Silver = Perak
Skinny = Kerus Kering
Sleep (Deep) = Tidor Lelap
Smart (Appearance) = Kachak, Lawa
Soft = Lembut
Sour = Asam
Spicy = Pedair
Stingy = Kedekut
Straight = Terus
Straight (Hair) = Tak Keriting
Strong = Kuat
Stupid = Bodoh
Suffer Greatly = Terokshan
Sweet = Manis

T

Talkative = Bijak
Tall = Tinggi

T Continued

Tasty = Sedap
Tasteless = Tawair
Tender (Meat) = Noa
Thin = Kurus
Throbbing Pain = Mengentak
Tired = Leteh

U

Ugly = Burok
Unexpected = Tak Sangka
Unlucky = Malang
Untidy = Semak

W

Weather = Chuacha terang (Bright weather)
White = Puteh
Wide = Lebair

Y

Yellow = Kuning
Young = Mundah

Zeng He was greated with great ceremony.

NOTES

Baba Malay or Chakapan Baba or the Baba language was born when Chinese traders sailed down to Southeast Asia and intermarried with the local women. A mix of Hokkien and Malay, Baba Malay went into decline after WWII as many Peranakans were killed.

This is one of the reasons why there are no Baba Malay equivalent to some words today. When in doubt English words are often used.

Another reason for the decline is language integration.

Baba Malay has two registers:

      1. Alus i.e., a refined form that women tended to speak
      2. Kasair i.e., a coarser version practised by men.

Baba Malay tended to be spoken rather than written so there are many variations in the spelling e.g.,

      kreja or kerja (work)

When in doubt I referred to Kenneth Chan's *Baba Malay For Everyone - A comprehensive guide to the Peranakan language* as well as William Gwee Thian Hock's *A Baba Malay Dictionary.*

Baba Malay is also sadly considered an endangered language.

Let's do our best to change this!

Bibek Theresa

In return, he imparted knowledge of building and planting.

About the Author

Theresa Fuller

Theresa Fuller has always loved stories and story-telling, but it was not until the birth of her first son that she became a full-time writer. Her aim was to write stories about her culture: Southeast Asia.

Theresa was Head of Computing at various private schools in Sydney. She has also been a Higher School Certificate (HSC) Examiner and HSC Assessor. Her teaching degrees have seen her work in primary and secondary schools and at Kalgoorlie College in Western Australia.

Her first published novel in 2018 was *THE GHOST ENGINE*, a steampunk fantasy about the fictitious granddaughter of Ada Lovelace, the world's first programmer. Theresa has published two books on Southeast Asian mythology: *THE GIRL WHO BECAME A GODDESS* (2019) and *THE GIRL SUDAN PAINTED LIKE A GOLD RING* (2022).

In 2023, *WHERE CRANES WEAVE AND BAMBOO SINGS* a visual narrative textbook for children and beginner writers was published.

Coming in September 2024 - *EATING THE LIVER OF THE EARTH* - collection of the lost folktales of the mousedeer Sang Kanchel.

In 2020, Theresa lost many family members. She threw heself into researching her family history as a way to deal with her grief. This was when she discovered that the language of her ancestors - Baba Malay - was on the verge of extinction. As a writer, teacher and selfpublishing author, Theresa found herself in an unusual position - she was able to create the curriculum that was needed to help fill a vacuum.

The result is the **Baba Malay Today** series.

All in aid of saving the language.

www.theresafuller.com

Thank you for your support!

More Books in the Baba Malay Today Series

Book 1 - Interrogatory Part I   SAPA, APA, MANA *or*
WHO, WHAT, WHERE

Book 2 - Interrogatory Part II   AMCHAM, APASAIR, BILA *or*
HOW, WHY, WHEN

Book 3 - Conjunctions   TAPI, ABIS, PASAIR *or*
BUT, SO, BECAUSE

Book 4 - Prepositions   ATAIR, KAT, BAWAH *or*
TOP, NEAR, BOTTOM

Book 5 - Antonyms   ALUS, KA, KASAR *or*
DELICATE, OR, COARSE

Book 6 - Essence   CHAKAPAN BABA ATI *or*
THE HEART OF BABA MALAY

Book 7 - Poetry   CHAKAPAN BABA PANTUN *or*
THE POETRY OF BABA MALAY

Book 8 - Idioms   CHAKAPAN BABA IDIOMS *or*
THE IDIOMS OF BABA MALAY

Note: In Standard Malay, the word 'hati' means the liver/heart i.e., the core. The word 'ati' in Baba Malay actually means 'liver'. Heart is 'jantong'. But phrases such 'kind-hearted' and 'evil hearted' in Baba Malay are 'ati baik' and 'ati pekong' respectively. Not 'jantong baik.' Hence, I have used 'ati' to express the meaning of the word 'essence' or the core.'

married some of the local women. And stayed.

Dear Reader,

Thank you for the purchase of this book.

Please help us spread the word as we try to save our language.

If you wish to learn more, here are some books:

> *A Baba Malay Dictionary by William Gwee*
>
> *Baba Malay for Everyone by Kenneth Y.K. Chan with Amelyn Thompson*
>
> *A Grammar of Modern Baba Malay by Nala H. Lee*
>
> *The Babas by Felix Chia*
>
> *Ala Sayang by Felix Chia*

In 2024, I will also be publishing a new series - New Peranakan Tales. These are bilingual and blended readers.

Let's all work together to save our heritage.

Bibek Theresa

Sydney, 25 of March, 2024

Coming 2024!!!

Books in the New Peranakan Tales Series

Gua Pi Keday

Satu Taon Jalan-jalan

I Went to the Shops

A Year of Walks

Want to know when my next book will be out?

Go to www.theresafuller.com

Join my newsletter!

And never miss out again.

www.ingramcontent.com/pod-product-compliance
Lightning Source LLC
Chambersburg PA
CBHW050305120526
44590CB00016B/2501